Cleave Notes on Communication
Copyright © 2014 by The Good Life Series Inc.

Dedication

To my husband, Ikem.

Foreword

Communication is such an important part of life but often overlooked until a major deficit is noticed. Many may not fully understand the power of our words and actions (verbal and nonverbal communication) and may not put much thought behind what we say to or about others. However, as Christians, we know that the bible teaches us just how powerful our words can be.

Our words can justify us or condemn us (Matthew 12:37). They can bring us joy (Proverbs 15:23), or corrupt and dishonor us (Matthew 15:11). What we say can either build up or break down the soul of whomever we are speaking to (Proverbs 15:4). The consequences of what we speak are so great that our words can lead us to ruin or save our lives (Proverbs 13:3).

-The Power of a Praying Wife,
Stormie Omartian

Like so many of you, I have not always been the best communicator. In fact, as a young adult, I was often told that I was bossy. Over time, I have come to realize that effective communication is not only verbally expressing yourself but it also encompasses listening, respect, cooperation, and congruent actions. God has blessed me with being able to further my education to better understand human behavior and connection and I am truly honored that I was asked to contribute to such an outstanding and inspiring piece of work that addresses such an important topic.

I have known the author, Ladisa Onyiliogwu, for over 20 years. She has always expressed confidence in her faith and has never been shy when it comes to sharing God's word with others. As an undergraduate college student, she continued to maintain her bond with God by joining the college's gospel choir and becoming active in her aunt's ministry. She regularly invited those of us who were new to the city to join her at her aunt's ministry on Sunday mornings so that we too could continue on God's path in the absence of our parents. Ladisa has also shared her gifts that God has given her in a gamut of ministries. She has worked with the homeless, opened a dance studio committed to allowing children and adults to praise God through their creative talents, sang in multiple choirs, led a youth ministry and praise team, and is currently a Sunday School teacher. She is not limited by a single denomination and has a greater understanding of how God's word is universal and is for all people.

Ladisa has always shown a passion for helping/teaching others. Her spirit is genuine and so bright that people are drawn to her wisdom and knowledge. I am not surprised that she decided to share her knowledge with others in the form of a God inspired self-help book, however, I am a little surprised it took her this long! In Cleave Notes on Communication, Ladisa has joined her love for God, knowledge of the scripture, and her life lessons to create a wonderful tool for Christian wives to help us understand how to improve our communication within our marriages. In other words, she has created a communication instruction manual for wives to help us have a better chance at winning this game called marriage. This book clearly defines how to put God first in your communication with your husband.

Ladisa's ability to reach out to all women of God is evident in her work. She has written this book so that it is relevant to wives who are newly married, those that are veterans, and women who aspire to be in a Christian marriage. Marriage is constant work that never stops "as long as you both shall live." Therefore, wives should incessantly make efforts to improve their relationship not only with God but also with their husbands and understand that a successful Christian marriage is the unity of a husband, a wife, and God. Ecclesiastes 4:12 states, "Though one may be overpowered, two can defend themselves. A cord of three strands is not quickly broken."

During the early parts of my 13 years of marriage, I often approached disagreements with my husband with a demanding, my way or the highway type of attitude (yes I acknowledge that I lived up to the name bossy). I would talk, talk, talk until he saw things my way. And when I did not get my way, I would stop talking, yes complete silence (sometimes for days) in an effort to show him I was really angry. Was my silence effective? Was it Godly? No! However, there are times when silence is golden (and not just when you are in a movie theater). It is important to know the difference between a constructive silence, which is discussed in chapter 3, and a malicious silence that is used to punish our husbands. Why would I call the latter malicious? Malicious means spiteful, vindictive, mean, nasty, hurtful, cruel, and unkind. When your silence is done with any of these synonyms in its intention or you intentionally withhold your words, thoughts, feelings, and or affections from your husband, you are not doing what God has instructed us to do as Christian wives. Ladisa does an excellent job explaining not only silence but the complete roll of a wife through God's eye in this book.

Let us all commit to becoming better communicators within our marriages.

In Him,

Tisha M. Johnson, Psy.D.
Clinical Psychologist
Practicing in Decatur, Georgia

Table of Contents

Preface

Sometimes, when I think of the word cleave, I envision a hook locking into the roof of a fish's mouth. The more I picture this image, the more painful the thought becomes. Unfortunately, the same pain or discomfort of my mind's fish is equivalent to the burden some wives feel when it comes to the topic of communication.

It's interesting how the tone and intent of our words change over time after we say "I do." I never imagined that I would communicate anything other than sweet nothings to my husband after our wedding day. I thought that our marriage would be as melodic as the New York Philharmonic. But, for some reason, our relationship produced a lot of flats, not enough sharps and little harmony.

The Lord finally revealed to me that a major player in this orchestra called marriage is communication. To quote author and entrepreneur Susan Scott – "relationships are built or ruined one conversation at a time". I was unaware of how greatly my words impacted my husband and his desire for me. I had no idea that I was doing the opposite of what Genesis 2:24 charged my husband to do.

"A man shall leave his father and his mother, and shall CLEAVE unto his wife: and they shall be one flesh."

Our Heavenly Father takes words very seriously. His Word is the one thing that will remain after heaven and earth pass away. He expects us as wives to imitate His character and sentiment. We have to be as intentional and thoughtful about the words we use in our marriages.

To cleave is to adhere closely, stick or cling. This is God's intent for Christian marriages. Our husbands' internal charge is to cleave. Our internal charge is to compel our husbands to cleave. Through healthy, God-inspired conversations, we can help our husband carry out his charge given by our Heavenly Father.

This book is the first of the Cleave Notes series. It speaks to the hearts of married women about the importance of strengthening their marriage through their words. The only resemblance to this book and the infamous "Cliffs Notes" is this fact – you won't pass the test if you don't actually study the real book.

Each chapter is inspired by an aspect of "The Lord's Prayer" (Matthew 6: 9-13). At the end of each chapter is a formula for you to begin the process of adjusting your speech to God's word on a more consistent basis.

Regardless of your current marital state – lovey dovey, hot & heavy, or dull & estranged, God can meet you where you are. I believe He will fulfill His plan for your marriage if you are willing and obedient. The Great Conductor has written all the notes you'll ever need to have a harmonious relationship with your husband. Take your time as you read Cleave Notes on Communication and just follow His lead.

C h a p t e r   O n e
"Our Father, Who art in Heaven...."

HEY SISTER!

The best template for prayer is given to us in Matthew 6:9-13 – 'The Lord's Prayer'. But did you know that this example can also be used as the perfect model for healthy communication in a marriage? Our Heavenly Father has given us everything we need in His word to have harmonious, melodic, and intimate marriages. It's simply up to us to follow His conducting and play the proper notes.

Communication, although hard to believe, is pretty basic and consists of a beginning, middle, and an end. The Lord's Prayer has this exact same structure.

- Beginning – 'Our Father'
- Middle – Requests, needs, supplications
- End – Closure with expectation

The beginning of communication establishes who is involved. When it comes to the Lord's Prayer - it's just you and Jesus. In marriage - it's you and your husband......and of course, Jesus.

If you're looking for a better way to communicate with your husband, the beginning of the Lord's Prayer is a great place to start. The words "Our Father, which art in Heaven" establishes our focus and who we're attending to in prayer. The phrase defines the parties involved in the communication process. It sets up an atmosphere of communication between a sender and a receiver. Too many times, Christian women forget about the receiver part and send, send, send prayers, requests, and plenty of pleading to the Father with no interest or space allotted for Him to respond back.

Prayer is not a one way street with you and God – neither is the communication between you and your husband. In order to improve the manner in which you communicate with your husband, focus simultaneously on your Father in Heaven. By focusing on Him while conversing with your husband, then your motives will remain pure, your tone will remain in check, and you will gain the outcome (or at least come close to the outcome) of the conversation that was initially desired.

There's something else that I must share about the beginning of a conversation. Only The Lord can read your mind - your husband can not. As much as we want him to, he just can't. Don't assume that he knows what you're talking about during the communication process. There's an acronym that I use to help me remain clear when talking to my husband.

B.A.R.

Beginning   Assumptions   Realities

There are times when I have a conversation with myself - in my head (and will later continue that conversation with my husband.) Problem. My husband has no clue about the BEGINNING of my thought, much of the context is missing and misunderstanding, misinterpretation and confusion are likely to ensue. So remember, always begin at the beginning of your thought with your husband. Don't leave him out.

Assumptions are unhealthy and can lead to poor outcomes in communication. Let's role play for a minute:

Wife: "You know, my dad cleaned my car every Saturday morning when I was a teenager."

Husband: [Crickets]

Later that month, the wife's car is still dirty. She thinks, "And no, I'm not going to wash it! Why should I? My dad always cleaned my car. My husband is supposed to clean my car too!!"

Now, she's angry, erroneously comparing her husband to her dad and creating hostility in their marriage. By the way, her husband has no clue why she's so frustrated with him.

This communication issue could have been avoided if she would have verbally communicated her desires and expectations in a loving manner instead of ASSUMING that her husband was going to clean the car every Saturday like her dad did.

Realities - The end of the story is that she finally disclosed her assumptions, suffered through some choice words (nothing too bad) from her husband and they eventually got over that roller coaster. Today, her husband expresses his intentions of cleaning the car – although it doesn't always manifest into a REALITY! But, at least the wife understands and knows that he is thinking about it.

Isn't that what we want - our husbands to think about our needs? The Word says that "I know the thoughts that I think toward you, saith the LORD, thoughts of peace, and not of evil, to give you an expected end. (Jeremiah 29:11). The Lord's thoughts towards me are precious (Psalm 139:17).

When we acknowledge our Father at the beginning of the Lord's Prayer, we have assurance that He is going to hear us and our prayer (I John 5:14-15). We can expect an interaction, an exchange of information and truth. The same can be applied to our husbands. Acknowledge him at the beginning of your conversation. Mind your manners and remember simple etiquette…..hello, good morning, Hi husband. Can I talk to you for a moment?

In tribute to my favorite musical, The Sound of Music, wives, 'Let's start at the very beginning….a very good place to start'.

Your Personal Cleave Notes

REFLECT on Genesis 2:24 - *Therefore shall a man leave his father and his mother, and shall cleave unto his wife: and they shall be one flesh.*

_____

_____

_____

_____

_____

REQUEST revelation from The Lord concerning your communication style.

_____

_____

_____

_____

_____

RECORD your thoughts and any promptings of the Holy Spirit and additional scriptures that you can meditate on for the next 3 days.

_____

_____

_____

_____

_____

RECITE the following prayer:

Lord, I acknowledge that my change of words,
conversations, and thoughts begin with you. Help me
to focus my attention on things that are eternal. I
believe you will cause me to triumph in this temporal
task of communication here on earth. I commit my
tongue unto you and I pray that you will keep it.
Thank you for being mindful of me and the words I
speak. You are my ultimate focus and I worship you.
In Jesus' Name, Amen.

_____

_____

_____

_____

_____

_____

_____

_____

_____

_____

_____

_____

_____

_____

C h a p t e r   T w o
"Hallowed be thy name...."

HOLE-Y VOWS

Everything about the marital relationship should be holy - even your conversation. As wives, you should desire that your words are holy.

Stop now for one minute and think about yesterday's conversations. What words did you speak to your husband? What words did you *not* speak to him?

The Bible says in James 3:11 "Can both fresh water and salt water flow from the same spring?" You can't expect salt water and fresh water to flow from the same cistern. Do we as wives speak kind, loving words one minute and damaging, cutting words the next?

Let's put it another way – Are you kind (FRESH) to others and short (SALTY) with your husband?

Recall our focus in communication – our Heavenly Father. He is Holy. His ways are unlike ours (Isaiah 55:8-9). The Lord's ways are magnificent, perfect and sure. We are created in His image and are to imitate His character of holiness.

The second stanza of 'The Lord's Prayer' is "Hallowed be thy name". This is translated as "let your name be sanctified". Sanctified comes from the original Latin word sanctifico which means "to separate and set aside". When Jesus gave us the ultimate example of prayer, He wanted us to first acknowledge our Heavenly Father and then to understand that His name is separate, different, unique, and unlike any other name on this earth or in heaven. Through this understanding, we are able to reverence and identify even more with His nature of holiness. The outcome of this realization is that we can make the holiness of God's name known.

We accomplish this through emulating the character of Christ. The Lord has given us the pinnacle example for engaging in conversation with our husbands - Holiness. This focus purifies not only our speech but the place of initiation - the heart.

Luke 6:45 says "…Out of the abundance of the heart the mouth speaks." Your surroundings can influence the matters of your heart. Whatever is taking priority in your life becomes a part of your thought life. Every human being is comprised of four states – mental, physical, emotional and spiritual. The thought life stems from the mental state. To quote Christian preacher, philosopher, and theologian Jonathan Edwards, "The ideas and images in men's minds are the invisible powers that constantly govern them." The thought life grows and develops in the heart, goes back to the brain and commands the body to take action.

For example: your environment could be saturated with 3 little children - ages 11 months, 3 years, and 7 years of age. These little ones have needs and they fulfill their needs through the source called "Mommy." Your ears hear their concerns; your eyes see their needs, the demands and their joy. Their words sink into your heart and you are filled.

Nothing else can enter because they have consumed your heart. So the thoughts of your heart are geared towards this environment.

When there is a need from this environment, your brain commands your body to take action immediately. Now what if there is another factor in the environment called "husband" that has a simultaneous need? What is the brain going to do?

If you have not intentionally placed your husband as a priority in your heart, or set him apart in his rightful place, he will not be a priority in your words or actions. In no way am I suggesting that you ignore the needs of your children. I am saying that you must acknowledge our Heavenly Father's order for the family (God – 1st; Husband – 2nd; Children – 3rd). Scriptures do not exactly lay out this order; however, Deuteronomy 6:5 clearly establishes the first order – "Love the LORD your God with all your heart and with all your soul and with all your strength." Ephesians 5:22 admonishes wives to 'submit to your own husbands as unto the Lord.' The wife's second priority is to her husband which places children as the next priority.

Not only is having an understanding of the familial order important, knowing your husband's place is critical. Your husband is the head of your household. He is the earthly priest of your family. The position of husband is a position of respect and authority. Your place as indicated in Titus 2:5 is to be a keeper at home. This vocation is one of strength and order and is not to be minimized or demeaned. You set the tone in your home with your husband and children. You oversee the health and wellbeing of your family. Your position requires that you show respect while simultaneously knowing your calling as a joint heir with your husband to Christ. The absence of respect, honor and order in terms of your husband's position can be detrimental to your marriage. If you don't have a correct understanding of position and authority in your marriage, you will have an unhealthy approach to your marital conversations.

You are required as a Christian wife to honor your husband's position through thoughts, actions, and words. Hopefully, you don't ponder ill thoughts towards your husband in your heart. If you do, unholy words are sure to follow. The principle is tried and true. As a man thinketh in his heart, so is he (Proverbs 23:7).

In contrast, building holy thoughts in your life is the needful thing. Be ye holy for I am holy. How can we be holy? How can we be holy communicators?

Romans 10:17 says "So then faith cometh by hearing and hearing by the word of God." I recommend that you read the following scriptures aloud, hear them and allow them to sink deep in your heart:

- John 6:43
- Philippians 2:14
- II Thessalonians 3:12
- Proverbs 14:1

If you are struggling with the words that you are reading right now, take a minute to bind the spirit of pride according to Matthew 18:18 and loose the spirit of humility. James 4:6 says that God gives grace to the humble but opposes the proud. God knows your situation. He sees everything (why do we forget this truth?). Even if your husband is not behaving as the earthly priest God ordained him to be, you still have an obligation to walk worthy of the vocation to which you were called (Ephesians 4:1). The blame game won't fly in heaven. When you're called to give an account of your role as a wife, your husband won't be there with you. You still have to be accountable for your actions and words and do everything through the power of the Holy Ghost to fulfill your role.

You want to be holy in your communication, not unhole-y. This is not a typo. Being unhole-y means you're full of holes and can't accept the words imparted to you right now because of unforgiveness, constant use of profane words, or pride.

One of the quickest ways to mend these holes is to use the threads of praise and worship. This is supernatural, super-strength thread that will piece together your heart's desire and stitch it together with healthy words. When you adopt praise of our Lord Jesus Christ into your daily walk, your communication to your husband is impacted. The Holy Spirit will either remind you that everything you say should be to the Glory of God. Or the Holy Spirit will convict you because everything you say is recorded by God.

When you communicate to your earthly priest, always remember your Heavenly Priest. As you acknowledge the holiness of God and glorify Him in

25

your speech, your marital conversations will be strengthened.

Your Personal Cleave Notes

REFLECT on Colossians 3:2. Consider the holiness of God and all His wondrous glory. Meditate on His goodness and love for you.

_____

_____

_____

_____

_____

REQUEST revelation from The Lord concerning any holes in your life that affect your ability to be a holy communicator.

_____

_____

_____

_____

_____

RECORD any words or conversations that do not reflect the holiness of God. Record the opposite of those conversations, practice and recite them aloud and apply them in your next interaction with your husband.

_____

_____

_____

RECITE the following prayer:

Heavenly Father, You are holy and righteous. There is none else like you. I love you Lord and am so grateful that you created me in your image. You have given me the ability and the power to speak words of holiness to my husband. I commit my tongue unto you today Father. Your word promises that whatever is committed unto you, you will keep until the day of Jesus Christ. Replace my carnal thoughts and words with yours. Allow me to operate and communicate in a spirit of Holiness.

In Jesus' Name I pray, Amen.

_____

_____

_____

_____

_____

_____

_____

_____

_____

_____

_____

_____

_____

"Thy kingdom come…"

THE KING'S DOME

Envision "The Lord sitting upon His throne high and lifted up, and His train filling the temple." Isaiah 6:1 visually paints a picture of God in all His splendor and glory in His spiritual kingdom. Now, imagine standing in front of Him. Ask yourself one question - what would you do?

Would you:
- Bow down
- Worship
- Praise
- Be silent
- Stand in awe

Everything mentioned above involves some form of communication - verbal or nonverbal. If you communicated to your husband one or more of the examples given, you would see a tremendous positive change   in   your   marriage.

Consider the first example - Bow down. No, I'm not telling you to bow down at your husband's feet -

he may pass out! When I think of bowing down, I think of reverence and honor. Do you reverence your husband in conversation? Are you using listening skills, exercising silence, and self-control while communicating with him? Or are you interrupting, disregarding what he says and talking loudly? Remember, God's word admonishes us to respect and honor our husbands. Reverence is part of that.

What about Worship or Praise? When was the last time you praised your husband? Philippians 2:3 says "Do nothing out of selfish ambition or vain conceit. Rather, in humility value others above yourselves." As wives, we can lift up our husbands and give complimentary words that will build their confidence. This act of praise and love towards your husband is a tool to aid him in cleaving more to you.

What speaks volume but doesn't utter a word? Silence. Ah, it's golden, right? It can be as valuable as gold if used in the right way. Even though communication moves back and forth between you and your husband, sometimes you have to allow the conversation to just flow one way. Especially in challenging talks. At times, you may have to adhere to silence and allow the quiet space between the two of you to diffuse problems. Pray for the fruit of self-control when you are tempted to issue a tongue-lashing or word-whacking. Sometimes you have to just get still and be silent.

Stand in awe. The term stand in regards to God's spiritual kingdom depicts stillness and attentiveness. Once we enter His spiritual Kingdom, we will definitely be in wonder, amazement, and awe. Our Lord will be our focus as we enter into His presence. Nothing else will matter.

If you're reading this book, you're still here on earth and not in God's kingdom yet. This means there is still time for you to practice similar acts towards your husband. Do you give him undivided attention when communicating? Or are you distracted? At times, my husband will move in close to me while he's speaking. He'll touch my shoulder when I'm not giving eye contact. He'll shift to my path of vision to make sure that I am listening. I remind myself to stand still and listen. This way, I communicate to him that I care and am attentive to him.

Another way to practice standing in awe with your husband is to acknowledge when he does something wonderful or out of the ordinary. My husband is not a handyman. On the contrary, he will pay someone to change a light bulb. Just kidding! However, one day he decided to fix our shower drain. This was extraordinary and totally out of his comfort zone. Not only did I tell him thank you, I verbally expressed how proud I was of him. He did not receive this in a condescending manner. Instead, he thrived from my encouraging words and support. The next time your husband does something awesome, tell him.

These are just a few examples of how God's heavenly kingdom can influence our communication. However, I would be remiss if I didn't explain what the earthly kingdom is comprised of and what Jesus meant when He stated this particular phrase.

David Cronic is a writer who posted a profound article in 2009 entitled "What do we mean by 'the kingdom of God?' He said that when Jesus spoke of the Kingdom of God in the first century, he was referencing the restoration of God's Shekinah glory which was no longer housed in the earthly temple. Jesus was teaching about another temple that would house the Holy Spirit. According to Mr. Cronic, for Jews in the first century, the kingdom of God not only meant the restoration of the Shekinah glory, but the return from exile and the defeat of Israel's national enemies.

Let's talk briefly about the restoration of God's Shekinah glory. Once we received Jesus Christ as our Lord and Savior, our names were written in the Lamb's Book of Life and the Holy Spirit came to indwell us.

We are the temple of the Holy Ghost. As wives, we have to remember that the awesome, powerful Shekinah glory of God lives in us. Our bodies are essentially God's Dome. It is His dominion. We have the power and strength required to conduct ourselves in excellence, lovingly communicate with our husbands and display character that will compel him to cleave.

Mr. Cronic also wrote that the kingdom of the Triune God confers a reciprocal loving relationship, not hierarchical power. The kingdom of God offers "liberation, not domination. The kingdom of the Father, Son and Spirit is where justice and peace kiss (Ps. 85:10) and where all things are renewed (Rev. 21:5)."

Your marriage may not mirror this truth – right now. But I believe that we are to 'call those things that be not as though they were' (Romans 4:17). If there is a dominating spirit in which your husband lords his authority over you, don't fear. Don't fear intimidation or domination. Decree II Corinthians 3:17 out loud to yourself in your house! Say it every day if you have to. If Jesus declared 'Thy kingdom come', then it has to come in your life. And as a wife, it has to come to your marriage.

Jesus' referral to the kingdom of God, as stated earlier, dealt with the children of Israel returning from exile. But how do we cause exile in our marriages? One way is through poor communication. Exile is defined as the state or a period of forced absence from one's country or home. Proverbs 25:24 says "Better to live on the corner of a roof than to share a house with a nagging wife." You're not exemplifying the Kingdom of God if you are a nagging wife. And if you are, then you are the slow force behind your husband's exile. He does not feel comfortable in his own home. This is the opposite of what he is called to do – cleave. How can we compel him to return and be restored? As a wife, you can aid the restoration process through the communicated word of God. Apply the scriptures that I've shared thus far and continue using them daily.

The last explanation that David Cronic gives of the kingdom of God is that Christ has confronted evil and triumphed over it. This truth should be evident in our communication. So far we've talked about shifting our focus to God as we engage in conversations with our husbands (Chapter 1). We've also talked about the importance of holy thoughts that exemplify a Holy God (Chapter 2). Now, I'm asking you to think about your actions. Realize that you are living in the King's Domain triumphantly and rest in this truth the next time you converse with your husband.

Your Personal Cleave Notes

REFLECT on Colossians 3:23
Think carefully about the actions you display while communicating. Do they mirror God's kingdom or Satan's?

_____

_____

_____

_____

_____

REQUEST help from The Lord to reverence, listen and attend to your husband in a similar manner you would towards Him.

_____

_____

_____

_____

_____

RECORD new actions, words communicated and revelations for the next 3 days.

_____

_____

_____

_____

_____

RECITE the following prayer:

Father, I praise you for you are Holy, righteous and King of my life and my marriage. Forgive me for not glorifying you through my words and actions. Help me to remember that your kingdom provides fullness of joy and pleasures for evermore. You triumphed over Satan and his tricks and they will no longer impact my ability or will to love my husband as your kingdom dictates. I will trust you for strength and power to fulfill my role as a loving, faithful, kingdom wife. In Jesus' Name, AMEN.

_____

_____

_____

_____

_____

_____

_____

_____

_____

_____

_____

_____

_____

<u>C h a p t e r   F o u r</u>
"Thy will be done on earth as
it is in heaven."

HEAVEN ON EARTH

Yes, I know – I divided verse 6 (hopefully, you're reading along in Matthew 6: 9-13). But it was important that I focused on God's kingdom first. Now, we can talk about God's will for your life.

When Jesus prayed 'thy will be done on earth as it is in heaven, He knew that we needed to know what is God's will. I don't think He would have prayed this arbitrarily with the intent of confusing us or leaving us wondering…. 'what is God's will for my life?'

Thessalonians 5:18 is one clear example of God's will. "In everything, give thanks, for this is the will of God in Christ Jesus concerning you."

Do you communicate to your husband that you're grateful? Or are you always complaining? Are you like streams of living water or a slowly dripping faucet that just won't quit? God expects us to give thanks in everything. Even if your marriage is not on the upside of the roller coaster - you don't have an

excuse to complain. Notice I didn't say a reason.
There may be plenty of reasons to complain, but you
have no permissible excuse to complain. Why?
Because our Lord and Savior Jesus Christ has
provided our every need. He promised it. He can't lie.
He can't repent.

At times, marriage is hard. Communication in
marriage is harder. I attended a service where Max
Lucado was the speaker. He began his message with
the following statement:

*"You'll get through this. It won't be painless. But
God will use this mess for good. In the meantime
don't be foolish or naive. But don't despair either.
With God's help you'll get through this."*

He then followed up by asking – 'how could He
[God] have the audacity to say such a thing?' Yes,
there may be extreme hurt – lies, health problems,
adultery, abuse, bankruptcy. You name it. 'But God
will get you through it all'. The key phrase is "but
God." Anything before a "but" becomes void. As you
trust God in the process of improving your
communication, you will be able to place all of your
problems, complaints, arguments, contentions, anger,
rage, and whatever else in front of "but God." God
can take anything bad and make it good. This is a
promise for those who love Him. Because of this

truth and the fact that He will deliver us sooner or later, we can thank Him now.

Thanksgiving enables us to focus our minds on Christ who will get us through any storm in life. I'm reminded of a song my youth fellowship choir would sing in the 90's at Providence Baptist Church in Greensboro, NC – 'Through it all' by Andre Crouch:

Through it all,
Through it all,
I've learned to trust in Jesus,
I've learned to trust in God.

Through it all,
Through it all,
I've learned to depend upon His Word.
Verse 3
I thank God for the mountains,
and I thank Him for the valleys,
I thank Him for the storms He brought me through.
For if I'd never had a problem,
I wouldn't know that He could solve them,
I'd never know what faith in God could do

This song didn't mean a hill of beans to me at the age of 14. I had no idea about what I was singing. But, as I reflect on those words today - oh, I experience chills up and down my spine. How

gracious is the Lord. I thank Him for everything in
my life – the good and the bad. I gain strength and
confidence to continue to carry on and carry out what
he has called me to do, especially as a wife.

In addition to thanksgiving, God's will for us is
obedience.

Who are we as wives not to do the will of the
Father? Jesus did not think it was beneath him to
take on human flesh, dwell with us, die for our sins,
and be resurrected again. That was God's will. Jesus
even acknowledged it:

"My food is to do the will of Him who sent me
and to finish His work" (John 4:34). "I can do
nothing on my own. As I hear, I judge; and my
judgment is just, because I seek to do not my own
will but the will of him who sent me" (John 5:30).

Obedience is God's will. And, obedience is
better than sacrifice. Don't sacrifice your marriage
because you can't obey God's instructions to you.
Don't sacrifice treasures laid up in heaven because of
disobedience. Don't sacrifice your testimony or your
character because of disobedience.

Still not convinced? Or maybe you really don't
know how to carry out His will. Philippians 2:13
says "For it is God who works in you, both to will

and to do his good pleasure." Pastor George Anthony of Atlanta, GA explained this scripture. He said 'even when you don't have a desire to communicate with your husband, God will give you the 'will'! Even when you don't know how to communicate with your husband, God will show you 'how'!' God's word leaves no room for excuses.

One other will for your life is to be a good wife. Ephesians 4:1 says "I therefore, the prisoner of the Lord, beseech you that ye walk worthy of the vocation wherewith ye are called." Well, what vocation was Paul talking about? If you are married, he was talking about the vocation of a wife. Simple. When you walk worthy of your job duties (as a wife), you please the Lord. When you please the Lord, you carry out his will for your life here on earth.

I don't want you to think that I glossed over the phrase 'As it is in heaven.' We know that the plan of salvation has been accomplished. This occurred when Jesus ascended into heaven and sat down at the right hand of God. That act declared that it was a done deal! Everything that Christ came to do on earth was accomplished when He returned to heaven. In the New Living Translation bible, John 17:20 says "I am praying not only for these disciples but also for all who will ever believe in me through their message." Jesus was talking about you. He was telling His disciples that [there will be some wives two thousand years from now who will believe in me, so I'm praying for them now. They have access to my kingdom and power because of what I'm doing now]. Go ahead and shout!

Our King is so wonderful that He empowered us before the beginning of time to be good wives. By ascending to heaven and pouring out His holy spirit on us, we can carry out His will.

At this point in the book, you have information on how to intentionally focus on your husband and communicate to him with holy thoughts. As you reciprocate information or ideas during a conversation, you are engaging kingdom principles to help you express your point of view. You should also be recalling God's purpose and will for your life. This may seem like a lot. But it's not.

Begin practicing your new skills with a simple conversation about washing the dishes or taking out the trash. Start with the easy conversations and practice. In time, these skills will develop in you and begin living in your heart. Before you know it, they will flow out of your mouth and your husband will start cleaving more. Just keep practicing.

Your Personal Cleave Notes

REFLECT on the following scriptures concerning
God's will:

Philippians 2:13   Psalm 40:8

I Peter 2:15   Colossians 1:19

Psalm 143:10   Jeremiah 29:11

_____

_____

_____

_____

_____

REQUEST help from The Lord to speak words of life
and truth to your husband.

_____

_____

_____

_____

_____

RECORD every job duty you have as a wife. Then,
ask the Holy Spirit to help you walk worthy in every
task that you recorded.

_____

_____

_____

RECITE the following prayer daily for the next 3 days:

Lord, I will not rebel against your will for my life.
Father, I desire to please you in everything that I do,
think and especially the words that I speak. Help me
to learn and know your will for my life as a wife. As I
grow in the knowledge of you Lord, I will grow in my
ability to speak kind, loving and encouraging words
to my husband.
In Jesus's Name, AMEN.

_____

_____

_____

_____

_____

_____

_____

_____

_____

_____

_____

_____

_____

C h a p t e r   F i v e
"Give us this day our daily bread"

YOU ATE WHAT?

Raise your hand if you're an Over-Planner! For all of my procrastinators ……..well you can raise your hand tomorrow.

Regardless of the former or latter, both groups are guilty of not seeing today and all that God has provided in this very moment.

As an over-planner, you may tend to skip over the 'here & now'. If not careful, you can become consumed with the 'next' in your life and miss out on the beauty that God has prepared for you today.

Psalm 118:24 says "This is the day that the Lord has made. Let us rejoice and be glad in it." The 'Day' in this scripture refers to the death, burial, and resurrection of Jesus Christ. But because of that day, I can rejoice in this day. The word says that God's grace and mercy are new every morning (Lamentations 3:23).   Philippians 4:19 says "My God shall supply all my need according to His riches in glory by Christ Jesus." This is a promise from God that He will provide your every need.

Did you ever wonder why it didn't say needs? I often have. I believe that God wants us to truly rely on Him daily for what we need. He knows what we need as a wife, mom, worker, or business woman.

Our first need as a wife is the daily bread, the word of God. Jesus said, "I am the bread of life." He teaches us through the sacraments of communion to eat of his body and drink of his blood. As we eat of the bread of life every day, our hearts become filled with God's truth, His ways, and His wisdom. The manner in which you eat will determine the impact on your conversation. As you fill yourself with God's word, you will overflow with words of truth. Luke 6:45 says "Out of the abundance of the heart, the mouth speaks." If you take heed to the scripture "give us this day our daily bread" and feast on God's word, then your conversation will reflect the character of Christ. Your mouth will speak what is in the heart. Can you imagine how your marriage will grow by applying this common principle?

This scripture in Luke is also for our protection. When you are provoked by the enemy to say malicious, critical, sarcastic, or hurtful remarks to your husband, the abundance of God's word in your heart will cause the opposite to come out. Even though your head may desire to speak venom, your heart will cause 'Rivers of living water' to flow.

The daily bread is such a great analogy to the elements of communication which are words, tone of voice, and nonverbals.

Let's review the first element – words. How do you select your words when communicating with your husband? Is there a hidden agenda or motive? Do you use factual information or concoct information to benefit you? Are your words cutting or are they encouraging? Compare your answers to God's Daily Bread. Does He have a hidden agenda, false information, cutting, or degrading words for you?

Think about the tone of voice you use when communicating with your husband. One way to help your husband cleave to you through communication is to speak from the heart or to display sincerity. My favorite scripture is Philippians 1:10 – "..that I may approve those things that are excellent, that I may be sincere and without offense til the day of Jesus Christ." Paul was encouraging the believers to grow in the love and grace of Christ. He was teaching that the best way to carry out God's mission of discipleship and spreading the good news was through sincerity. Your tone should convey concern, interest, and true sincerity when communicating with your husband.   Let's conduct the same exercise by comparing God's tone with yours. How does He speak to you daily? Is it threatening? Is He insincere?

What are examples of nonverbals? Eye contact, dress and clothing, visual aids, animation, emotional content, energy, strength, concept of others, listening, setting, body language, attitude and confidence, silence. There are so many more examples of nonverbals, but I'd like to discuss a few of the ones just mentioned in detail.

Did you know that your dress attire and clothing communicate volumes? Of course you did. When you're not physically motivated to love and be intimate with your husband, what do you do? Put on sweat pants, a wrinkled tee, or maybe leave on the coke-bottle glasses? On the other hand, a beautiful, silky lingerie adorned before your husband requires no comments from you.

How is your eye contact when communicating with your husband? Is it shifty? Is it fiery or direct and interested? Eye contact helps you to connect with your husband. It lets him know that you are present, even in a difficult conversation. Even in a hurtful, trying discussion that involves pain and tears.

What does the daily bread say about body language? Though shalt roll thine eyes, shruggeth

48

thy shoulders, foldeth thine arms and smacketh thy teeth! On the contrary. Read Numbers 6:24-26. In verse 25, "the Lord makes his face to shine on you and be gracious to you." Revelations 1:16 says…. "His face was like the sun shining in all its brilliance." How magnificent. Imagine standing in the sun and feeling its warmth shining on you right now. Wouldn't it feel calming, soothing and revitalizing? God's face shining upon you is so much greater than the sun's warmth. His face illuminates our environment, it alters the atmosphere; it is reassuring and loving. I pray that we will all learn to represent our Heavenly Father's shining face as we encounter and communicate with our husbands. Our ultimate desire is to be like Christ.

Listen, I can give you tips on how to communicate with your husband this day. I can give you tips on how to correct your tone and nonverbals this day. But, if you don't read the word of God for yourself this day, if you don't seek His shining face, you won't succeed in compelling your husband to cleave. Ask The Lord to give you –today- His word and His will for your life and marriage. Don't talk about how you messed up yesterday. Don't push tomorrow. Just focus on today.

When I was pregnant with my son, I realized that my appetite was quite odd. Unlike my first two pregnancies, I was able to inhale anything that I placed my eyes on at any time of the day. I had no issue with nausea and didn't care about the weight gain. I would eat Taco Bell quesadillas with fries and an hour later - cereal and muffins. It seemed as if every combination of food made sense. I was so emboldened that I named myself Combo Girl. That's right. Any combination of food I could imagine, I would make it or buy it and eat it.

I never second guessed what I would eat. It was just the norm. As Christian wives we also have a norm regarding our diets. I'm sure I'm not the only combo girl when it comes to eating our daily bread. I take a little II Corinthians 5:7, add Ephesians 4:1 and sprinkle Salt 62:8, excuse me Psalm 62:8.

It doesn't matter how you feast on God's word. Any combination will do. God is waiting for you and ready to speak to you about your marriage. He's ready to teach you through his bread how to communicate with your husband. He is ready to show you His best and how your husband can and will cleave to you. Read the word and read it every day.

Your Personal Cleave Notes

REFLECT on your favorite scripture.
Record it below and think about how it relates to
your marriage.

_____

_____

_____

_____

_____

REQUEST help from the Lord to read the word every
day. Ask Him specifically for the best time and place
where you can not only read but hear from Him.

_____

_____

_____

_____

_____

RECORD key phrases or words that stand out to you
as you read his word. Review these at the end of
each daily reading session.

_____

_____

_____

_____

_____

RECITE the following prayer:

Lord, Thank you so much for your word. It is precious to me. It is life, health and healing to all my flesh. I know I need to spend more time in your word and pray that you will help me in this area. Show me when I can set time aside for you. I need you more and know that as I connect with you, learn from you and read about you, then my marriage will benefit and grow. I trust that you will speak to me and teach me how to be a better communicator. I love you so much. In Jesus' Name, AMEN.

_____

_____

_____

_____

_____

_____

_____

_____

_____

_____

_____

_____

C h a p t e r   S i x
*"And forgive us our trespasses as we
forgive those who have trespassed against us"*

SIMPLE, BUT NOT EASY

Oh, the 'F' word. Some of us view forgiveness as
if it was a bad word. You know it's not. I know it's
not. There are so many scriptures that end a promise
with the admonition to Forgive. It is expected of us
from God. It is a directive to us from God.

Another favorite scripture of mine is Mark
11:23-24:

23 "For verily I say unto you, That whosoever shall
say unto this mountain, Be thou removed, and be
thou cast into the sea; and shall not doubt in his heart,
but shall believe that those things which he saith shall
come to pass; he shall have whatsoever he saith."

24 "Therefore I say unto you, What things soever ye
desire, when ye pray, believe that ye receive them,
and ye shall have them."

But, how often do I gloss over vs 25?

Mark 11:25-26 (KJV)
25"And when ye stand praying, forgive, if ye have
ought against any: that your Father also which is in
heaven may forgive you your trespasses. 26But if
you do not forgive, neither will your Father who is in
heaven forgive your transgressions."

Why did He put that there?! I was fine with
the decreeing and declaring, naming and
claiming – but forgive. It seems a bit out of
place, right? Wrong.

Our Heavenly Father is a just, loving, and
forgiving God. This is what makes Him so unique
and the only, true, wise, and living God. He forgave
our sins through his son Jesus Christ. We have
access to the throne of grace because of this
forgiveness. We can enter into heaven because we
accepted Jesus as our Lord and Savior and asked for
forgiveness.

So who are you not to forgive others? It is
unholy to harbor unforgiveness in your heart. Recall
Hallowed be thy name. God's name is to be
hallowed. He is holy. You have to be holy. You
don't want to be hole-y, i.e., full of holes, empty and
unable to receive God's grace because of
unforgiveness.

Only you and the Lord know what you've been through. Only the Lord knows what your husband did to you. Do you think that some things happen and the Lord's response is, "Hmm, didn't see that one coming!" NO. God knows everything about you. Everything. He knew you before you were in your mother's womb. He loves you so much. His love doesn't change because of something your husband did or did not do.

As much as it hurts, there is no greater hurt than God's creation turning its back on Him. But He forgave us. And so we must forgive our husbands. We have to forgive ourselves. Our conversation should not be prideful or stubborn to the point where we can't apologize. Your husband may never apologize. Some of you are looking for him to do right, I know. But, you're also looking for him to remove the hurt. You're looking for him to release you from the pain and anguish that he's caused you. He Can't Do that! Only God can. And ye are complete in Him (Colossians 2:10).

Women sometimes have to be the stronger vessel in the forgiveness area. I'd like to share with you a few points that I learned from Walt Latimore that will explain what I mean.

I Peter 3:7 says "Likewise, husbands, live with your wives in an understanding way, showing honor to the woman as the weaker vessel, since they are heirs with you of the grace of life, so that your prayers may not be hindered." There is no contradiction between what I said and what Peter said. I said stronger vessel, Peter said weaker. But trust me, it's the same.

Walt Larimore expounded on the Greek word 'weaker'. The ancient Greek word can literally refer to someone that is sickly or unwell. But Pastor Larimore believes that God attributed the woman's design described in secular Greek which has a richer meaning. The form of the word describes the most fragile and valuable artwork, the most delicate and elegant china, the finest and most expensive vases or the most elegant crystal. It is a term used to describe any other dainty, delicate, luxurious ethereal, subtle and extremely rare gift.

Pastor Larimore also explained that 'woman wasn't made like a man was made, she was built.' The woman is built for rehabilitation, built for beauty, stability, and durability. We are built for aesthetic appreciation but also inwardly built to withstand, sustain, and last. You and I both know that there is some inexplicable strength that occurs on the inside of us when we face a hardship or trial.

God made you durable and strong for a reason. After you face overwhelming struggles, you are still called to forgive and you have the strength to do so. Our problem is not a lack of strength. You know now that you are not weak. Your problem at times is disobedience.

So what if your husband committed an outrageous mistake and knows it but refuses to admit that he was wrong? So what if you are wrongly accused of something that he perceived but it had nothing to do with your original intent. Be the example. Forgive.

I have to admit that marriage at times feels like a roller coaster. One day, we're coasting and enjoying the scenery. All of a sudden, we're on a downward spiral that took us by surprise. That downward spiral often times is unforgiveness along with pride, resentment, anger, frustration, or a refusal to communicate.

There was a time in my marriage when I was the only one to forgive. I was the only one to say 'I'm sorry'; the only one to ask for forgiveness. Our roller coaster moved to the higher rail each time I did, but would spiral further downward if I didn't. At no time did my husband apologize in the past. Getting him to ask for forgiveness was like pulling hens teeth….hens don't have teeth.

It was hard for me and I started to resent my husband. I thought, 'Why won't he apologize? He's the one that did wrong. He's the one that hurt me.' But nothing. His actions became my excuse to resent him more and harbor unforgiveness in my heart. Instead of heeding to God's directive to me to forgive, I was focusing more on how my husband would not forgive.

Unforgiveness breeds hostility, anger, negative emotional reactions, or curt responses. If we're honest, unforgiveness can completely halt the communication process. Think about it. If you have not forgiven your husband for a wrong, do you really want to talk to him? If you have to talk to him, aren't your words mean, ugly, hostile, angry, or emotional?

As Dr. Charles Stanley, Senior Pastor of First Baptist Church in Atlanta, Georgia always says, unforgiveness doesn't harm the other person. It only harms you. It can mentally, emotionally, spiritually, and physically harm you. I have even experienced a fiery, stabbing sensation in my heart as a result of not forgiving my husband.

The Lord knows that if we don't obey His command to forgive, there will be no way for us to communicate properly with our husbands. It's impossible.

The great thing about this Christian life is that we serve the God of impossible. Scripture states 'what is impossible with man is possible with God.' If you're having a hard time forgiving your husband, quote this scripture over and over again. You may have to recite it to yourself before beginning a conversation with him. As you release your hurt and forgive, your speech will begin to soften. Your words will become more sincere and loving. Your obedience will glorify the Lord and He will cause your husband to cleave.

Your Personal Cleave Notes

REFLECT on Galatians 5:24.
Consider past conversations or actions that have resulted in unforgiveness. Record those incidents that you just can't seem to forgive.

_____

_____

_____

_____

_____

REQUEST for the Lord to cover you with His heart of mercy and ask for you to display the same mercy and forgiveness to your husband.

_____

_____

_____

_____

_____

RECORD revelations and promptings from the Holy Spirit regarding your new walk in forgiveness.

_____

_____

_____

_____

_____

RECITE the following prayer:

Father, sometimes I can't let go of the unforgiveness. But your word says in Micah 6:8 that I am to do what is right, to love mercy and to walk humbly with you. Father, please forgive me for walking in pride and disobedience. Help me to honor you by forgiving my husband. I release all hurt, pain and anguish in my heart. I lay it at your feet and trust that you will fill my heart with love, joy and peace. I forgive my husband. In Jesus' Name, AMEN.

_____

_____

_____

_____

_____

_____

_____

_____

_____

_____

_____

_____

Chapter Seven
"And lead us not into temptation"

The Ultimate Trainer

What are you tempted to say in conversations with your husband? Are you tempted to omit information in order to avoid a fall out later? Are you tempted to gossip? Are you tempted to scrutinize? You may be tempted to provoke him with sarcasm. You may even be tempted to not talk at all when there is a need to talk. When tempted, no one should say, "God is tempting me." For God cannot be tempted by evil, nor does he tempt anyone; but each one is tempted when, by his own evil desire, he is dragged away and enticed." (James 1:13-14)

There is a great quote on a hermeneutics website that says the following:

"The trainer that brings us into the arena to fight is not the opponent we face."

Did you know that God is our trainer? A trainer is someone who teaches you the skills you need to be able to do something. Don't you need the skills to communicate better with your husband? If not, you wouldn't be reading this book. The skill of communication is a very important one and is the foundation for healthy, happy marriages. God, our trainer, wills and allows things to happen in our lives. He is not tempting us, He is training us. Each day is an opportunity for your trainer to build skills in you.

My day job is an adult trainer. Prior to instruction, I begin the class explaining the goal (or purpose) and the objectives to achieve the goal. I suppose that our Heavenly trainer does something similar. Can't you see Him standing at the front of the classroom with a clicker and PowerPoint presentation welcoming us to His class? I envision He would say something like this:

Good morning and welcome to the 'Becoming a Better Wife' Training Course. My name is Alpha and Omega, Counsellor, Rose of Sharon, Heir of all things, the Just One, King of Kings, Lamb of God. But you can call me Jesus. I will be your facilitator today.

The goal of this course is to teach you, mold you, and develop you into the wife that I have called you to be.

This goal will be achieved through the following objectives: Reading my word, studying my word, and daily tests.

63

The outcomes of this course will be:
- To build up your most holy faith
- To work out your soul salvation
- To hear the words well done thou good and faithful servant

As your trainer, I am going to allow certain things to happen in your life. You will be faced with temptations by the tempter. When you do (not if), don't become alarmed. Remember, I faced temptations as well by that same tempter. So, let's get started with class.

We can be comforted in knowing that our Heavenly Father can identify with the temptations that we face. This is proven in Matthew 4:1-11 (just a few chapters prior to the scripture focus of this book). If the tempter tried to tempt Jesus, then we can expect temptations in our marriage including our marital conversations.

Before we talk about the tempter and his schemes, let's define temptation. The Merriam-Webster dictionary defines temptation as: something that causes a strong urge or desire to have or do something and especially something that is bad, wrong, or unwise.

Have you ever noticed that you're not tempted to do something to which is easy to say no? Why not?

Because it's not really a temptation. When Satan tempts us in our marriage, it's generally not going to be a cake walk. It's going to be (or has been) subtle but strong enough for us to consider following his lead. And he is the one who will lead us to use our words for evil not for good towards our husbands. This trickster and deceiver will use any opportunity available to infiltrate our communication.

When we fall into temptation, we become a pawn used by the enemy to destroy our husbands. By giving into his schemes, we become rebellious against our role as wives and against God's will instead of resisting the enemy and fleeing.

The temptations in your marriage are no different from what others experience. But God is faithful. He will not allow the temptation to be more than you can stand. Whatever the temptation, God has said that He will provide a way out (I Corinthians 10:13). Listen carefully – Flee! Take the way out! Don't just sit there….look at the open door…..but still do what you want to do….and repent later.

Don't fall into rebellion. Recall chapter 5 when we discussed the strength of a wife. We can be so strong to the point where not only do we use our words for evil, but we become the tempter of our husbands.

Does this last sentence remind you of someone famous?

Eve's way out was right, left, front, or sideways. She was in a garden. All she had to do was run! But she didn't. She was tempted by Satan and then she went and tempted her husband. She repeated the exact same words that Satan said to her and adopted them as her own.

I'm sure you realize that every thought you think and every word you are tempted to say is not always your own. Scripture supports this statement.

II Corinthians 10:5 says "Casting down imaginations, and every high thing that exalteth itself against the knowledge of God, and bringing into captivity every thought to the obedience of Christ." Every thought is not your own, but every thought must be brought under the subjection and obedience of Christ.

Any thought that goes against the will of God or counters what you know about God is of the devil. You must exercise your authority in Christ and take captive the thought. Make sure you do this quickly before the thought is expressed through your words. This principle is critical when you are tempted to think ill-will toward your husband. I'm not saying that every poor thought about your husband comes

66

from Satan. You're sometimes the culprit. But when tempted, flee. Look for your door out.

The door may be silence, a smile, a prayer, a breath, or Matthew 18:18. The Lord may compel you to bind the negative, poor thought and replace it with the mind of Christ.

There is one additional point that I need to make regarding our words and temptation. Not only are we tempted to talk poorly to our husbands, we are tempted to talk about our husbands to others. This form of temptation is generally a result of hopelessness, anger, resentment, frustration, or despair. All of these are excuses.

You may feel like you need an outlet to talk about the pain and troubles you're experiencing in marriage. I understand. Christian counselors are excellent. Use them as a resource. But neither your girlfriends, co-workers nor your mother needs to be a dumping ground for you to complain about your husband. We've all been tempted at one point in time. I've even justified my actions by equating them to 'sharing my frustrations'.

This is dangerous territory.

Woman of God, you are called to help your husband cleave to you, not tempt him to leave you. I cannot stress enough how important it is for you to get this principle into your head. Let it sink down deep into your soul.

This book is for your marriage. It can apply to you while you are talking with your husband or while you are talking to someone else about him. Don't be tempted to talk about your husband to someone else.

So what would be possible outcomes of this type of temptation? Use any of these three words (deprave, corrupt, and degenerate) to complete the following statement:

I _____ my marriage when I give into the temptation to talk negatively about my husband.

I'm sure you can come up with plenty of other words to fill in this blank. Note: these three words are synonymous to evil.

Let's change the words around a bit:

I _____ my marriage when I do not give into the temptation to talk negatively about my husband.

What words come to mind? Build, strengthen, preserve, fulfill my vows to, cover, protect....

The list can go on and on. As we cover, build, strengthen, and protect our marriage, our husbands are built, strengthened, covered, and protected. This will cause him to love us more and cleave more.

This portion of the Lord's Prayer admonishes us as wives to hold our tongues. When you're with a girlfriend or a close aunt or a confidant and are tempted to talk ill of your husband (or you may begin talking about his character flaws, or sharing your woes which implicate your husband for not doing something), pray immediately and ask the Lord to show you the way out.

Your Personal Cleave Notes

REFLECT on Matthew 26:41
Consider incidents or occurrences that provoke you
to fall easily into temptation.

_____

_____

_____

_____

_____

REQUEST that the Lord opens your spiritual eyes to
recognize temptations and ask for help to exit
through the door of escape.

_____

_____

_____

_____

_____

RECORD examples of how you avoided temptations
over the next week.

_____

_____

_____

_____

_____

RECITE the following prayer daily for the next 3 days:

Dear Lord, I know that you are not my tempter. On the contrary, you love me and want an intimate relationship with me. Father, I pray that you will give me spiritual wisdom and insight so that I might grow in your knowledge. I pray that you will open the eyes of my understanding of how to resist temptations by the enemy. I desire to walk with you and please you in everything that I do. I love you in Jesus' Name, AMEN.

_____

_____

_____

_____

_____

_____

_____

_____

_____

_____

_____

_____

_____

<u>C h a p t e r   E i g h t</u>
'But deliver us from evil'

Open Book Test

I did it again, but I had to. It was necessary to break the scriptures in parts and show the root cause of temptations. This chapter will devote our focus on the entire phrase: "and lead us not into temptation, but deliver us from evil."

Do you remember waiting to take a test and praying that your teacher will announce at the beginning of class, "This will be an open book test." In my academic experience, I probably took two, no more than three tests like this. I wish there had been more. Oh well.

The great thing about our Christian life is that all of the tests we face are open book! This chapter is a great example of how God provides the answer for temptation. Here's the question:

1. When faced with temptations to speak evil
    toward your husband, what should you do?
    a. Weigh the consequences before making
        a decision
    b. Commit the sin and repent later
    c. Pray for deliverance

Why do we fail so many of these open book
tests when the answer is right there in front of us?

When you do select the right answer, God will
reward you (but it may not be in your own timing).
In some instances, you will receive an immediate
deliverance from the tempting thought. On other
occasions, you may have to continue to pray 'deliver
me Lord' over and over again. Either way, the Lord
will deliver.

Our words can be cutting or soothing. They can
be good or evil; life or death. Proverbs 18:21 says
there is power of life and death in the tongue. They
that love it will eat the fruit thereof.

I've been guilty of speaking evil to my husband
and to my marriage. I even speak evil to myself,
sometimes. However, this is not God's will for my
life or yours. One of the most fitting answers to the
open book test of temptation is Ephesians 4:29: "Let
no corrupt communication proceed out of your

73

mouth, but that which is good to the use of edifying, that it may minister grace unto the hearers."

Do your words minister grace or minister resentment and unforgiveness?

There is power of life and death in the tongue. They that love it will eat the fruit thereof (Proverbs 18:21). No, this isn't a typo. I wanted to quote this scripture again and connect it in a different way. For, after the Holy Ghost has come upon you ye shall receive power (Acts 1:8). To do what? Power to trample on serpents, scorpions and every evil work of the devil (Luke 10:19). We have to use our words to counter the attacks of the enemy.

Your marriage, my marriage, every Christian woman's marriage is under attack by the evil one. Why? Because Satan is our foe. Foes don't want anything good for you. Our foe throws fiery darts. Our foe steals. Our foe destroys and tries to kill. Hmm, that rhymed.

But God is greater in you than our foe that is in the world (I John 4:4). If we have a foe, it means that we are in a battle. Our loving Lord has already equipped us with everything we need to fight this battle. It is your job to fight the fight of faith (II Timothy 4:7). It is also your job to know who you are fighting…..and it is not your husband. Your husband is not the enemy. Satan is.

Say this three times – 'My husband is not my enemy.'

If you have been using your words to speak evil towards your husband, stop it now. The best way to be delivered from evil communication is to speak God's word OUT LOUD. Pick a scripture. There are plenty in this book. By now, you have over 20 scriptures to which you can refer. Say these scriptures aloud daily.

Speaking the scriptures aloud will:

1. Increase your faith.
    "Faith cometh by hearing and hearing by the word of God" (Romans 10:17)
2. Strengthen your marriage.
    "Fear not. Neither thou be dismayed. For I am your God. Yea I will strengthen thee, I will help thee, I will uphold thee with my righteous right hand." (Isaiah 41:10)
3. Empower you to stand for your marriage.

Your weapon in this fight is faith in God shown through your actions and your words. But they cannot be carnal words. They have to be mighty through God….(II Corinthians 10:4). In every war, there is a strategy for fighting. Jesus gave us tactical information that we can use to be successful in communicating good (not evil) to our husbands.

The LORD is my rock, my fortress and my deliverer.... (Psalm 18:2). He told us from the beginning of time that we would not be able to walk away from evil or flee from evil by ourselves. It is only through His power that this can occur. Colossians 1:13 tells us that in one swift move through the obedience of Christ, we were delivered from darkness and transferred into God's kingdom.

If you have not passed this test yet, then perhaps your words on occasion have a flavor of bitterness when speaking with your husband. Or, you may have such an uncontrollable rage that you'd prefer not to talk to him at all. You may possibly have a stronghold in your life that is nurturing pride and creating violent hostility. The kingdom of darkness thrives on strongholds. Silence or a simple prayer won't do. The only way to get set free from a stronghold is to be delivered from it. Remind yourself that you are no longer in the kingdom of darkness. Speak the word of God, pray without ceasing and declare deliverance for your marriage as He promised.

Your Personal Cleave Notes

REFLECT on Psalm 139:23
Have there been any test in recent days where you
have spoken evil to your husband or about him to
others?

_____

_____

_____

_____

_____

REQUEST help to commit your tongue to the Lord
and practice using His word when prompted to speak
evil.

_____

_____

_____

_____

_____

RECORD any evil thoughts that enter your mind
when communicating with your husband on the left
side of the following 'T Chart'. On the right side,
record the opposite of that thought. Apply Matthew
18:18 to every line. For example, if the first evil
thought is 'judgmental' and the opposite is humility –
then pray this prayer: Lord according to your word, I
bind the judgmental thoughts that I think towards my

husband. I loose a spirit of humility in my heart as I speak to him.

Evil Thoughts when communicating	Holy Thoughts

RECITE the following prayer:

Father, You revealed to your children that Satan is a defeated foe. He has no power in my marriage or my speech. Heavenly Father, I commit my tongue unto you and I know that what is committed unto you, you'll keep it. I decree that my marriage is healthy and whole. I will obey you and speak life to my husband and to myself. Thank you for delivering me today, In Jesus' Name, AMEN.

_____

_____

_____

_____

_____

_____

C h a p t e r   N i n e
"For thine is the kingdom the
power and the glory forever amen."

After Today

Everything that you have belongs to the Lord. This includes the communication between you and your husband. This was affirmed earlier in Chapter Three. God has dominion over everything. Your problem is that you sometimes forget this truth. He is the one that has the power to cause your husband to cleave more to you. You just have to be a willing vessel. II Corinthians 4:7 says "But we have this treasure in earthen vessels, that the excellency of the power may be of God, and not of us." There is a supernatural power that lives in you right now and gives you the ability to communicate effectively to your husband. This is essentially what Cleave Notes on Communication is all about.

Don't you hate when books end? I do. Some endings leave me feeling happy, sad, joyous, frustrated, angry, or empty. There may be a sequel or two but that's pretty much it. This book will even have a few sequels, but at some point in time, the series will end.

There was a movie released in 1984 called the 'Never-ending Story'. It was a bit bizarre, full of imagination, and by far my favorite movie as a child. Well, you and I have the privilege of our own never ending story released at the beginning of time. It's not a movie, but a living book. Not only can we read it daily, we're in it, and we personally know the author. We can ask the author questions, we can prod His mind, and find out what he meant by this or that. We can read the never-ending story over and over again and it will always have a totally different effect in our lives.

Matthew 6:13 of the never-ending story says "…For thine is the kingdom, the power and glory forever amen."

Remember that your marriage resides in the King's domain. Everything about your marriage belongs to the Father. Trust Him to watch over His word to perform miracles in your married life. Your task is to continue communicating the principles of God's kingdom to yourself and to your husband.

Rely on God's power and strength when speaking with your husband. If you feel that you can't do some or any part of the techniques presented in this book, ask the Lord to help you. Psalm 62:11 says that Power Belongs to God. That same power lives in you. Exercise it. Use it.

Your speech should always glorify God. Of course, you may have been a part of conversations that did just the opposite. You may even be on the downward spiral of the roller coaster which threatens to end your marriage. Don't fear. Praise and glorify the Lord. Don't walk by what you see. Stand in faith and trust that God will take you from glory to glory as you obey and apply His word. God has a mandate of eternal glory and you're a part of this mandate. You will be a glory in the earth and so will your marriage.

The term 'Forever' should give you a sense of peace. You can rest in knowing that God has your marriage in the palm of His hand for the rest of your life. Forever is also a charge to keep practicing communicating God's way. Practice makes better. You can't give up. Don't get tired. Don't quit.

This last phrase of the Lord's Prayer reminds you of your focus. It's not about you, it's not about your husband – it's all about the Lord. What is His will for your life? What does He want you to do and say? How does He want you to interact and communicate?

I hope Cleave Notes on Communication has helped you to begin answering these questions. The techniques in this book are not original. They are

81

ancient but not antiquated. They are supernatural,
they are life; they are simply God's word.

So what happens after today? It's up to you.
The Bible is the actual textbook that you need to read
and study. Cleave Notes is just an accompaniment.
After today, I believe you will hear the Lord's Prayer
in a different way. After today, I believe that you
will approach communication with your husband
from God's perspective.

My prayer for you is summed up in the
following melodic note:

*Give me a love for you Lord that grows stronger
every day,*

*Let this love shape me and change my walk and my
ways,*

*May my husband know you and the power of your
might,*

*To be a mighty man of God who walks by faith and
not by sight,*

*May our marriage wax strong in love and desire,
Daily knitted together through trials and fire,*

Let my words be the cistern of encouragement,
sincerity and love,

May I speak only life and peace that comes from you
above,

As Christ loves the church, I believe that my husband
will love me,

And together we will walk and to me forever, he will
cleave.

Your Personal Cleave Notes

REFLECT on the three scriptures in this book that
have resonated with you most. Think about how your
communication has changed and will continue to
improve by applying them to your daily
conversations and thought life.

_____

_____

_____

_____

_____

REQUEST that the Lord continues to soften your
husband's heart as you communicate in a new way to
him.

_____

_____

_____

_____

_____

RECORD successes and testimonies of how your
husband cleaves to you as a result of using God's
word in your conversations.

_____

_____

_____

_____

RECITE the following prayer:

Lord, I am grateful to be in your kingdom. I am in awe of your power and glory. You are a magnificent God and I praise you. You reign over all things and I praise you. Help me to apply your words in everything I think, say and do. Bless my marriage Lord through the power of your Holy Ghost. Help me to be obedient to your will. And I pray that my husband will cleave more to me as you have ordained. I love you so much and glorify your Holy Name. In Jesus Name, Amen.

Notes

p. 21   **"The outcome of this realization"** "What
Is the Biblical Meaning of
sanctification." Christianity Exchange
Bible. N.p., n.d.

p. 32   **"David Cronic is a writer who posted"**
The Cry: The Advocacy Journal of Word
Made Flesh vol. 11, no. 2 "Word Made
Flesh." Word Made Flesh. N.p., n.d.

p. 62   **"A trainer is someone"** "Pioneers in
Dictionary Publishing since 1819." Collins
English Dictionary. N.p., n.d.